EDGE
BOOKS

Video Games vs. Reality

FANTASTIC
WORLDS

THE INSPIRING **TRUTH** BEHIND POPULAR
ROLE-PLAYING VIDEO GAMES

BY: THOMAS KINGSLEY TROUPE

CAPSTONE PRESS
a capstone imprint

Edge Books are published by Capstone Press,
1710 Roe Crest Drive, North Mankato, Minnesota 56003
www.mycapstone.com

Library of Congress Cataloging-in-Publication Data
Names: Troupe, Thomas Kingsley, author.
Title: Fantastic worlds : the inspiring truth behind popular role-playing
    video games / by Thomas Kingsley Troupe.
Description: North Mankato, Minnesota. : Capstone Press, 2019. | Series: Edge
    books. Video games vs. reality | Audience: Age 8-14.
Identifiers: LCCN 2018006072 (print) | LCCN 2018006710 (ebook) |
    ISBN 9781543525779 (eBook PDF) | ISBN 9781543525694 (hardcover) |
    ISBN 9781543525731 (paperback)
Subjects: LCSH: Military art and science—History—Medieval, 500–1500—
    Juvenile literature. | Military art and science—History—Medieval, 500–1500—
    Computer games—Juvenile literature.
Classification: LCC U37 (ebook) | LCC U37 .T76 2019 (print) | DDC 794.8/2—dc23
LC record available at https://lccn.loc.gov/2018006072

Editorial Credits
Aaron Sautter, editor; Kyle Grenz, designer; Tracy Cummins, media researcher;
    Tori Abraham, production specialist

Photo Credits
Alamy: AF archive, 19; EA: Dragon Age: Inquisition image used with permission of
Electronic Arts Inc., 8–9, 11 Bottom, 28; Granger: Sarin Images, 11 Top; iStockphoto:
ands456, 10, duncan1890, 17; Newscom: HANDOUT/KRT, 21, Handout/MCT, 4–5,
22–23; Shutterstock: Aerovista Luchtfotografie, 16, Bidaj doo, 18, Captblack76,
Cover Middle, CreativeCore, Design Element, Dmitrijs Bindemanis, 12–13,
Dmitrijs Mihejevs, 14–15, enjoy your life, Design Element, Fer Gregory, 25,
FXQuadro, 7, Kiselev Andrey Valerevich, 24, Laslo Ludrovan, 6, Lukasz Szwaj,
Design Element, omnimoney, Design Element, Serhiy Smirnov, Design Element,
sezer66, 29, Vitalii Gaidukov, 27, Zoran Pavlovikj, 20

Printed and bound in the United States of America.
PA017

TABLE OF CONTENTS

CHAPTER 1

In the Hero's Boots

An icy wind whistles as you climb up to the cliff's edge. The heavy armor protecting you makes every muscle ache. At long last, you stand before the dragon's lair. Your hunt for the fabled **scepter** has led you here. Your journey has been long, and you would give anything for some rest. But you step forward, ready to meet your fate.

scepter—a rod or staff carried by a king or queen as a symbol of authority

Nearby you hear a deep, throaty rumble. Your chest plate rattles as a mighty roar shakes snow from the nearby trees. A giant frost dragon lands on a rocky ledge near you.

The wind from its enormous white wings whips the surrounding snow into a blizzard. The beast roars again and unleashes a blast of frost from its jaws. You dive to the side, narrowly escaping an icy death. As you stand once again, you pull out your battle-worn sword. You raise the blade above your head and sound a battle cry of your own. The ice dragon shall not best you! Not on this day!

Video games inspired by fantasy worlds and mythical monsters have enchanted gamers for years. The thrill of playing in a magical world keeps game designers working overtime.

Many video game developers look to **medieval** history to bring realism into their adventures. They've studied historical warriors, weapons, and armor to bring gaming heroes to life. History has also guided game designers as they create fictional kingdoms where players explore, live, and fight. Legendary creatures from fables and fairytales are also brought to life to battle players.

Get your trusty sword ready. It's time to explore the real-life history that has inspired the most popular fantasy role-playing video games.

medieval—having to do with the period of history between AD 500 and 1450

▲ Medieval knights and warriors used a wide range of weapons and armor to fight and survive in battle.

CHAPTER 2

Choose Your Own Adventurer!

Most role-playing fantasy games allow players to choose a character at the beginning of the game. Games can take hundreds of hours to complete, so most gamers carefully choose a character that fits their gameplay style. No matter what players choose, video games are full of characters inspired by real people in history.

Dragon Age Inquisition used with permission of Electronic Arts Inc.

Hand-to-Hand Heroes

Video gamers often play as soldiers or knights. These characters are inspired by real-world warriors. Knights first appeared in medieval Europe as hired protection for **nobles**. They were highly trained and skilled—and deadly in hand-to-hand combat. Later, knights became the soldiers that formed a country's main military forces.

Games like *Dragon Age: Inquisition* treat these warriors in much the same way. As real-world knights once did, players take an **oath** of loyalty to a kingdom or cause. Like the medieval knights they're based on, the champions in the game are fierce and deadly in combat.

FACT

The term "knight" came from the Anglo-Saxon name for a boy: *cniht*.

noble—a person of wealth and high rank

oath—a formal promise to do something, often naming God as a witness

Mighty Magic Users

Some players choose a more "magical" approach to their game experience. No fantasy game would be complete without the option to play as a wizard or **sorcerer**.

In early medieval times, people often blamed magic for things they didn't understand. Religious leaders said bad weather, disease, and natural disasters came from evil magic. They thought evil spirits possessed anyone who used magic. People suspected of using the "dark arts" were punished or even killed.

sorcerer—someone who performs magic by controlling spirits

FACT

The term "wizard" comes from the Middle English word *wys* meaning "wise." Wizards were once known as wise men, until the name came to mean "magic user."

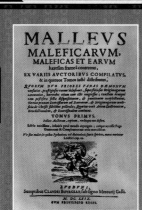
Witch Hunter's Handbook

The *Malleus Maleficarum* is a famous medieval text that focuses on magic. Heinrich Kramer wrote the book in the 1480s. It served as a guide for hunting and punishing suspected witches. The text also contains stories detailing Kramer's "successful" witch hunts.

Magical characters in video games are treated differently. Mages and sorcerers are often respected in the game world. In games such as *The Elder Scrolls V: Skyrim*, magic users are often considered to be the wisest people in the world. Magic users can cast lightning bolts or fireballs to destroy enemies. Or they can create magical potions to heal injuries.

Dragon Age Inquisition used with permission of Electronic Arts Inc.

⋀ In some video games, battle mages are the only ones powerful enough to stop the biggest, baddest monsters and villains.

Rule-Breaking Rogues

Some gamers like playing characters that don't always follow the rules. For these players, free-wheeling **rogues** might be the best choice. These characters look out for just one person—themselves.

Rogue characters in games are often **assassins**, thieves, or mercenaries. In the real world, assassins and thieves were often arrested or killed for their crimes. Mercenaries were paid for criminal deeds that their employers didn't want to do themselves. These activities often involved murder, raiding, and stealing valuable objects.

In the world of Skyrim, players can join a secret group known as the Thieves' Guild. The leaders of the group order the player to swipe treasures from towns, homes, and castles. There is also a secret order of assassins called the Dark Brotherhood. The group recruits the player to find and kill certain targets. But players need to be careful. As in the real world, if they're caught they'll spend a lot of time in prison.

FACT

The game *Thief* allows someone to play in the game's title role. The game is set in the late Middle Ages and follows the adventures of Garrett, a master thief who steals from the rich.

rogue—a dishonest person

assassin—a person who murders a well-known or important person, such as a king or president

CHAPTER 3

Realms of Possibilities

Every great adventure deserves a great setting. In most fantasy games, players journey across lands full of wide rivers, majestic mountains, and grand castles.

Welcome to the Kingdom!

Many fantasy games take place in kingdoms. A kingdom is a region of land ruled by a king or a queen, otherwise known as a **monarchy**. Kingdoms were one of the earliest forms of government. There are a number of them still found in the modern world such as Norway, Saudi Arabia, and the United Kingdom.

monarchy—a type of government in which kings or queens are the head of state and their children take their place when they die

The Legend of Zelda series usually takes place in the kingdom of Hyrule. It's a large kingdom filled with fortresses and fantastic creatures. The actual king of Hyrule is long gone, and the kingdom is almost always facing destruction. But in spite of their troubles the people there continue to go on with their daily lives. Just as in real historical kingdoms, the people of Hyrule grow their own crops, raise animals, and sell their wares in the market.

FACT

Ganon is usually the biggest threat to the Kingdom of Hyrule. He's known as the Great King of Evil and is quite powerful. He always seeks to obtain the mythical Triforce to defeat Hyrule and cast it into darkness.

outer wall

arrow slit

portcullis

moat

No Hassle Castle

Fantasy games are famous for featuring large castles. Real castles were usually used to help protect kingdoms from invaders and warring tribes. Early fortresses were built with earth and wood. But strong castles offering the best protection were made with stone. These large stone structures were built as early as AD 1066 in England.

Video game castles, such as Redcliffe Castle from the Dragon Age series, often include features found in real historical castles. Many times kings had castles built high on hills or cliffs that gave a wide view of the surrounding land. The high view helped soldiers spot approaching enemies.

Many castles were built with moats around them. These water-filled ditches made it difficult for enemies to get to and climb the castle's walls. **Portcullis** bars acted as an iron gate to block a castle's main entrance. Arrow slits were built into a castle's towers. The slits let archers fire on enemies while staying protected. And a castle's outer walls were wide enough to walk along. Soldiers could keep watch or fight enemies from above.

portcullis—a heavy gate of iron bars in the entrance to a castle that was used as an extra defense

CHAPTER 4

Monster Mash n' Bash

What makes a fantasy role-playing game fun? Monsters! Without monsters to threaten the world, a fantasy game would be pretty dull. Some monsters are giant creatures that can eat a character in a single bite. Others, like goblins and orcs, are there mainly to make life miserable for the hero.

The Little Guys: Goblins and Orcs

In German and British folklore, goblins were tricky, evil little creatures that lived in the dark. They liked to cause trouble. Descriptions of them vary in different stories. But over time, goblins became ugly, cave-dwelling creatures. Goblin bedtime stories were often used to scare naughty children into behaving and following the rules.

Unleash the Horde!

Goblin Commander: Unleash the Horde is an older game that lets the player control an entire army of goblins! Designed as a strategy game, the goal is to destroy the evil goblin forces before they take over the world. The Goblin Commander can order his horde to attack, or he can fight face-to-face with another goblin enemy.

folklore—tales, sayings, and customs among a group of people

In today's fantasy-based video games, goblins and orcs are easy targets. Game designers often follow the tradition of these beasties living in dark caves. Sometimes games show the simple villages these creatures build. Underground goblin towns often include small huts, simple tools, and piles of rotting garbage lying everywhere.

FACT

Orcs are a creation from J.R.R. Tolkien, author of the Lord of the Rings series. These goblin-like creatures have since appeared in many fantasy role-playing games.

The Big Guys: Trolls and Giants

When beating up weak goblins gets too easy, it's time to square off against something bigger . . . sometimes a lot bigger. Trolls are mythical creatures in tales from Scandinavia. They're usually tall, strong, and smelly. Trolls are nasty creatures with wicked teeth and claws.

Giants, on the other hand, are much larger and tougher versions of humans. But that doesn't keep them from enjoying people at mealtime. In several old stories, such as "Jack and the Beanstalk," giants like a nice breakfast of roasted humans.

Scandinavia—the part of northern Europe that includes Norway, Denmark, and Sweden

In video games trolls and giants are like the creatures found in old tales. Game designers challenge players with these man-eating monsters. Giants have super strength and can crush a warrior with one swipe of their huge clubs. Meanwhile, trolls are almost impossible to kill without using fire or sunlight. Unskilled players who stumble upon these deadly monsters usually meet a bad end.

FACT

Shadow of the Colossus was a very popular PlayStation 2 game that featured a wide variety of giants. Armed with only a sword, a young warrior named Wander fought and defeated several ancient giants.

Here Be Dragons!

Of all of the legendary fantasy creatures, none are more famous (or feared) than the dragon. These magnificent beasts are found in folklore from **cultures** around the world, including Europe and Asia. Dragons come in all shapes and sizes. Some have wings, while others look like giant snakes. Some breathe fire, and others have magical powers. There is no evidence that dragons ever really existed. However, past cultures may have thought dinosaur bones were the remains of dragons.

culture—the way of life, beliefs, customs, and traditions of a group of people

Inspired by Myths

Ancient Chinese mythology describes three species of dragons. They are known as *lung* (sky), *kiau* (marsh), and *li* (sea). Three similar dragons appear in *The Legend of Zelda: Breath of the Wild*. Dinraal the fire dragon flies around a volcano. Farosh is a dragon with electrical abilities and lives in a jungle region. Naydra is an ice dragon who can be found near a large ocean bay.

Gamers encounter several types of dragons in *The Elder Scrolls V: Skyrim*, including fire-breathing dragons, elder dragons, skeletal dragons, and more. The game won the best role-playing game award at the E3 Expo in 2011.

In *The Elder Scrolls V: Skyrim*, dragons play a huge part in the game's story. The main hero is known throughout the land as "The Dragonborn" and can use dragon magic. Many of the dragons in the game destroy towns and villages. But some dragons offer to help the hero on his journey. These helpful dragons are influenced by stories from ancient China where dragons often helped heroes. In some Chinese legends, dragons are heroes themselves and bring good luck to those in need.

Heavy Metal Merchandise

In medieval times it was impossible to defend a kingdom with good will, a smile, and a handshake. Knights and soldiers needed to carry weapons and shields to protect their country. Over time, tales grew of famous weapons carried by legendary heroes. These tales have inspired similar weapons in popular video games.

Swords of Legend

Throughout medieval history, few weapons were mightier than the sword. Several myths describe how legendary blades helped decide major battles. One such weapon was the famous "Sword in the Stone." It was said that whoever could pull the blade out of a giant rock would be made king. Men from all around tried but couldn't pull the sword free. But then a teenage farmer named Arthur gave it a try. The sword came loose instantly and Arthur was crowned the King of England.

Many popular video games include legendary swords in their stories. In The Legend of Zelda series, the young hero, Link, must pull the Master Sword from a similar stone. The sword has great power. But unlike Arthur, Link isn't made king for freeing the blade. He is tasked instead with rescuing Princess Zelda from the main villain.

One Sword or Two?

In many Arthurian stories, the "Sword in the Stone" and "Excalibur" are often thought to be the same sword. However, they are actually two different blades. The sword King Arthur pulled from the stone was broken during one of his many battles. He was later given the mighty "Excalibur" by the Lady of the Lake, a sorceress in the old tale.

Amazing Armor

Other than a weapon, a hero's most important equipment is his or her armor. Armor is designed to protect the body. The first armor was likely used during **prehistoric** times. Ancient people probably covered themselves with leather hides and helmets to protect themselves during hunts.

Knights and warriors began using full body armor in the 1200s. It helped protect them from weapon blows on the battlefield. Armor offered great protection, but it was heavy and clumsy. A full suit of plate armor could weigh up to 110 pounds (50 kilograms). Warriors wearing heavy armor often grew too tired to be effective in battle.

Armor is just as important in video games as it was in real life. Players won't last long battling deadly monsters and enemy soldiers without protection. Many games give players a variety of armor choices, depending on their playing style. If a character needs to move fast, then light-weight leather armor is a good choice. But if one needs to square off against a pack of trolls, then a full steel suit may be the best option.

FACT

Want your game character to go for a swim in that shiny new armor? Go ahead! In most games, swimming in armor isn't a problem. But don't try swimming across a river wearing heavy metal armor in the real world. You'll sink straight to the bottom.

prehistoric—belonging to a time before history was written down

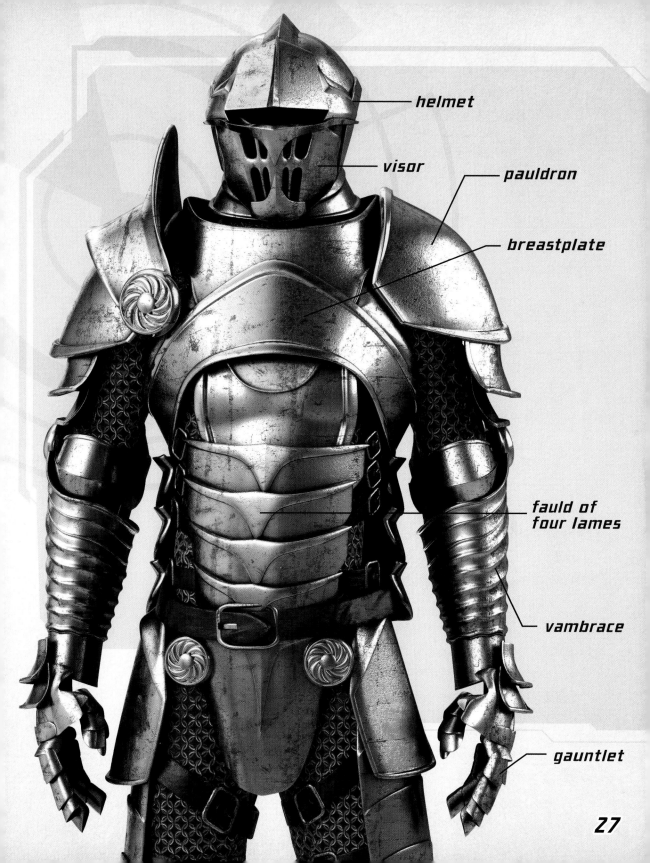

helmet

visor

pauldron

breastplate

fauld of
four lames

vambrace

gauntlet

27

Dragon Age Inquisition used with permission of Electronic Arts Inc.

Go Forth Adventurer, Your Quest Awaits!

It's amazing that the fantastic settings and creatures in video games are connected to real history and legends. Whether it's mighty castles or deadly monsters lurking in the shadows, medieval history has been an incredible inspiration for video game designers. However, game designers often exaggerate the facts to increase the drama, excitement, and action in a game. After all, escaping into a world unlike our own is why gamers pick up a controller in the first place.

Becoming a **virtual** wizard or warrior in a fantasy role-playing video game lets you live in that world. And fulfilling a quest can be very satisfying. Game makers know that basing games on real history can help spark players' imaginations. The realism draws players deeper into the story so they can enjoy becoming the heroes of their dreams.

virtual—not real; when something is made to
seem real on a computer

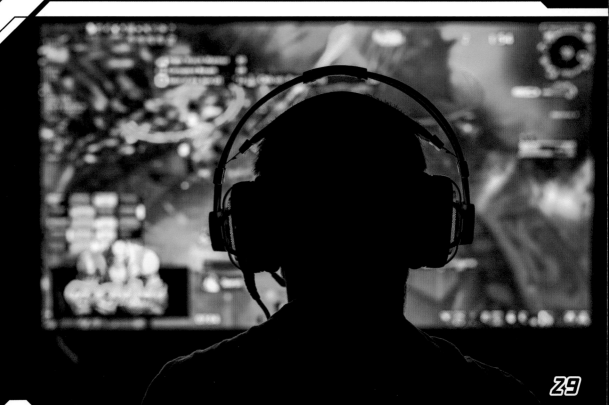

GLOSSARY

assassin (uh-SA-suhn)—a person who murders a well-known or important person, such as a king or president

culture (KUHL-chuhr)—the way of life, beliefs, customs, and traditions of a group of people

folklore (FOLK-lohr)—tales, sayings, and customs among a group of people

medieval (mee-DEE-vuhl)—having to do with the period of history between AD 500 and 1450

monarchy (MON-ahr-kee)—a type of government in which kings or queens are the head of state and their children take their place when they die

noble (NOH-buhl)—a person of wealth and high rank

oath (OHTH)—a formal promise to do something, often naming God as a witness

portcullis (port-KUHL-iss)—a heavy gate of iron bars in the entrance to a castle that was used as an extra defense

prehistoric (pree-hi-STOR-ik)—belonging to a time before history was written down

rogue (ROHG)—a dishonest person

Scandinavia (skan-duh-NAYV-ee-uh)—the part of northern Europe that includes Norway, Denmark, and Sweden

scepter (SEP-tur)—a rod or staff carried by a king or queen as a symbol of authority

sorcerer (SOR-sur-er)—someone who performs magic by controlling spirits

virtual (VIR-choo-uhl)—not real; when something is made to seem real on a computer

READ MORE

Lassieur, Allison. *Medieval Knight Science: Armor, Weapons, and Siege Warfare*. Warrior Science. North Mankato, Minn.: Capstone Press, 2017.

Sautter, A.J. *A Field Guide to Dragons, Trolls, and Other Dangerous Monsters*. Fantasy Field Guides. North Mankato, Minn.: Capstone Press, 2015.

Walker, Jane. *Knights and Castles*. 100 Facts You Should Know. New York: Gareth Stevens Publishing, 2015.

INTERNET SITES

Use FactHound to find Internet sites related to this book.

Visit *www.facthound.com*

Just type in 9781543525694 and go.

Check out projects, games and lots more at
www.capstonekids.com

INDEX